Expressions of
Love, Passion, and Intimacy

Compilations of Affection

Keep it Sexi

*Dedicated to the one whom
inspired me to write about love*

◆

My true "Kokaine"

From My Heart, to Yours

Inspiration comes from within. If you don't attempt to go after what you want in life, you will never get it. If you never try one step forward, you will always be bound to denial.

Through hard times and past difficult relationships, I learned that I possessed a wonderful gift within me. The gift of loving, and caring for other people's needs before my own. But I had to learn to start with me first. Once I did, I was able to love the one person I neglected most, me.

Point being, don't let anyone destroy your inner beauty or make you feel less of yourself. You have it in you, let it shine bright. And not just speaking to women because it can also be a man in the same shoes that lack that love and affection from their mate.

Remember they are the one that lack self-worth, happiness, and love for themselves. They would gladly destroy yours...IF you let them!

Trials and tribulations will come, but they will go, its how strong you overcome that proves your victory. Love is not easy, we all know this. But take time to figure out if they are really the right person for you.

If someone wants to be a part of your life they will make every effort to be in it. Why open the door to your heart for someone who doesn't make an effort to stay? Never feel as if you have to settle for less. I'm no expert but I have been through situations like anyone else and I know there is better out there.

If you are in search of love, wait for it to come. Never rush into anything, and take your time. If it doesn't come you may not be ready for it, or they may not be ready for you!

I wanted to speak a little from my heart to yours. I've fell many times, endured heartache and pain. But I never would have pulled through without constantly praying!

Let

Love be your Destiny

Destinee is Love.

Introduction

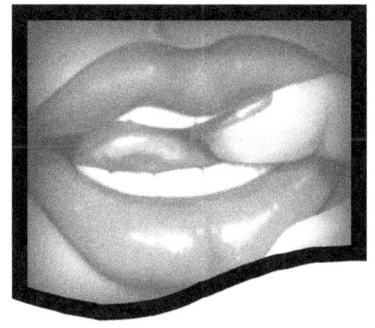

When I speak of love, I speak about it through many forms. Expressing how you feel for one another is not just a simple I love you. It goes beyond that. I'm no expert but I believe once you have found that "one", you would do anything and everything to satisfy their wants, needs, and desires.

Love, a powerful emotion, is a feeling that can't be explained, and controls your whole mind, body, and soul within. You ache for one sound of their voice, one glimpse of their face, or a loving embrace. These emotions are intense, erotic, very arousing, and definitely stimulating.

This is an unedited collection of my spoken words about love, passion, and affection. Once you have experienced it, you can understand the true meaning of it {Ecstasy}. Much Love!!

Wanting

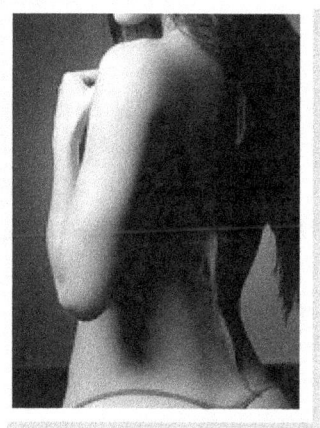

Yearning,

For your sweet thoughts, your soft words

recognition of my presence, your assurance

only I possess dominance to mentally

and physically arouse your flows within

I want to taunt you with sexiness

causing stimulating blazing desires of me

giving you mind blowing peaks of bliss

So intense!

How can we resist

this web of passion entangled

within our souls, thoughts and

desires. Wanting of each other

as we stand here gazing, fiercely

wondering what is about to begin

Staring,

Upon this perfect vision of a stallion

before my eyes, from your smooth

luscious lips to your ripped muscular

physique, eagerly awaiting a kiss.

One intimate kiss, leading to one intimate

touch. One intimate touch leading to

you wanting just a piece of me, just for

me to have one night of you.

I need you to want me until it hurts

I want to make you hunger for me

feast upon my weakness for you

Indulging as if you can't resist my

sweet taste of pleasure, candy coated

with heavy flows of caramel dew

Would you want me more than

just this moment? Because I desire you

in my dreams, in my thoughts, in every

waking moment wanting to amaze you....

Amaze you

With lust

With affection, better yet

With inevitable bliss of delight

Come to me, I want you in me for

you are the only one to bring my body

to light. Sensations from your lips kissing

my inner thighs...Tingles are raging

as you are embracing, grabbing, squeezing

my body oh so tight. In the darkness of

this room, I feel your love down the center

of my thighs. So thick, so enormously hard,

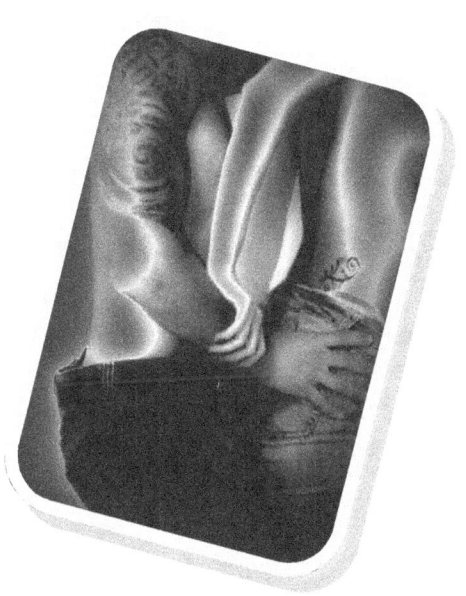

slowly dripping with the sweet

juices I want to taste badly on the tip

of my tongue, thirsty tongue

licking from bottom to top making you

produce more thus satisfying my quench.

Body heat is cultivating, fantasies

prevailing as I feel your tongue, so gentle!

Softly moaning and wanting more

working your way down to my spot.

Your lips and tongue motioning fast.

As I feel my clit swell, you move slower as if

you are waiting, waiting for me to give you

what you now want.. for me to spread my thighs

further and further, widened only for you.

Feel my back arch towards your mouth
so I can feel your hunger for me more
my body is blazing with fire like a volcano
reaching its peak ready to burst into a vicious
deadly flow.

Your urgent and demanding thrusts are
so intensive! I attempt to move my body
rhythmically for your pleasure, instead
screaming for mercy, my love sweet mercy!

I can hear you moaning my name from
the back of your throat. It's overpowering,
the strength of your grasps and blows to
my sanity pounding deeper and deeper
causing delusional outbursts of satisfaction.

Amazing,

More amazing than we had anticipated

Is this mercy I hear you shouting!

Screams and echoes of pleasing battle cries!

Driving together hitting harder

and faster I grab the sheets

you grab my hips

moving with each other's thrusts

I feel my thighs quivering

your legs trembling

bursting all over you as

you are blasting inside of me

Together, Mutually

Wanting

Adore your Embrace

From across the room, I look into your
caring eyes and realize that I am
completely safe. I feel the movements of
your body leading me to a sensual,
breath-taking embrace.

Standing here with you my love I confess
you have captured my heart
with your kisses, and stolen my body
with your desires. Your gentle hugs brings
warmth to my heart, sets my soul on fire.

I never felt embraces like this before
How are able to get inside and reach
the core? This is an amazing feeling
that we both adore, so astounding
forever wanting more. My body shivers
from the softness of your hands touching
my skin, I love your gently kisses to
my lips sending electrifying thrills within.

I love the warmth of your body covering mines. Softly caressing my body's outline there is a tingling feeling I try to hold inside. My love, can you feel the passion in my embrace to you. Feeling our hearts dance together as two, knowing you are here with me, emotions we can't hide.

I want this moment to last forever ending with never. Yours arms around me, touching me, securing me as if I was your most precious blessing,

Your aura so intoxicating, so compelling yet remarkably caressing. You are the only one I adore, the only one I want to feel embrace me so tight softly whispering
" You Always"

Every night, for the rest of my life.

Your Night, My Desire

Tonight is reserved only for you,
the only man I love and adore.
Passion, lust, and no time to waste,
just the two of us, close the door...

Candles lit burning their flame,
we're sitting here wrapped so tight,
Erotic games of slow licks and wet kisses,
to arouse desires of a quiet night.

The fireplace is burning bright,
and your aroma is smelling so sweet.
You look deep inside my eyes,
and kiss me softly on my cheek .

Come lay down on the bed,
your cologne is filling the air.
Your scent is making me go crazy,
as you're gently stroking my hair.

Your hot breath on my neck,
and the way you softly caress,
Gasps for air getting a lil' heavy,
as your body I slowly undress.

Feel my hands rubbing on you,
and the feeling of my wet lips.
You like the way I pull you closer,
gently grabbing on your stick.

Moving my hands gently over you,
exploring every inch of your skin.
Making passionate love to you,
until you beg for this night to end.

Our desires reaching their peak,
as I hold on tight to your arms.
You tell me do tha damn thing,
leaving me in a state of charm.

You're teasing parts of my body,
slowly & gently with your finger tip,
Thrusting 10 inches of passion in me,
You have me moaning biting my lip.

As we make love I close my eyes,
devouring our chaotic sounds,
I feel as if my body's floating
high up past the clouds.

With every thrust and movement
I come closer to my highest peak,
Our hearts are beating faster
boy you are making me weak.

My whole world shaking now
I slowly open my eyes,
To you holding me and saying
You will ALWAYS be mine.

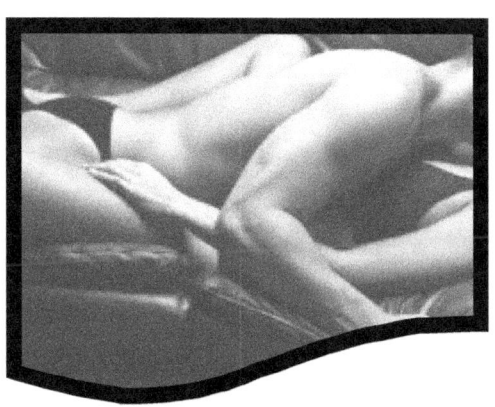

My Distant Love

Just to see you
Just to sense you
Just to touch you once more.

But I can't because distance dwells upon us. And even though I can't feel you, somehow I know you are here. A distance so fierce, so forcibly painful, a feeling so heart-breaking knowing I am here and you are there.

While you remain out of reach to me and possibly thinking of a beginning with someone there, I know I could be yours if you would just believe. We have short moments, but when we are together its as if you had never left.

Why is it I can't think, why is it I can't imagine my life without you, Is this true love? Why does my heart beat so fast at one little thought of you. Longing for your presence and sweet sexy smile, I wish you were here by my side, forever mines.

As I sit here reflecting on moments together, I can definitely state you have touched my life in ways unimaginable, taken my mind to higher levels, so high it shivers my soul thinking how gentle you were to my entire body.

You can't hide the shimmer in your eyes, the glow upon your face when you see me. And I can't deny the sparks you give me when I first see you. Every first moment we have is more exciting than the last.

You start with a gentle smile then slowly place your lips to mines. Kissing me passionately leaving me at a loss for words. You hold me so tight bringing my body so close to yours, sending shivers up my spine!

The force between us explodes as our bodies entwine. Grinding slow, so deep and hard, only you bear rights to the definition of ecstasy!

You confess your love by showing your tender affection and adorable charisma. These moments I hold close, and are dearest to me. You tell me that being here feels so right, wishing things could be.

Two different worlds, yet somehow we connect so well. From the moment we are together its as if we were made specifically for one another. Passion and intimacy takes over and binds our hearts as one.

But we both know this can not continue much longer. I have my life here, and you have yours there. And just like that our time ends and you're gone, once again.

It's been months, silence fell upon us. Getting over you is the hardest thing for me, I still love you without doubt. Though distance may have parted us, Never will I forget your distant love.

His Testimony

I feel its our last night together, I'll be leaving once the sun rises. I know that you will forever love me as I will forever and always love you.

I will share this night with you as if it were our last. I'm going to give you the most memorable night of your life so I will always be on your mind. I never want you to forget me.

Please forgive me love but not having you in my life everyday is killing me. I would rather let you go than to have you suffer as much as me. I don't want you to leave your life here, how selfish of me to ask of you!

I'm going to miss your love so much. You are and will be the only one to make my world complete. Filling this empty space in a lonely mans heart. I believe in destiny, I know we will be together one day. Maybe the timing is wrong but I can't see breathing life without you. Even if it takes a moment, I will never let another steal this place in my heart that belongs only to you.

So as we part and share our last kiss, I will bravely smile at you and tell you it will only be for a little while until we see each other again. I need time to make a way for you and me.

As the moment arise, you left my arms and my heart began to ache. Just the thought of not see-ing your beautiful face for however long is just too hard to retain.

Just as I drove away, it was that very moment I realized you were my everything, my one true love. Leaving you will be the hardest thing I've ever had to do. I will make a way for us to be together, bonded.....Never letting go.

Remember Me

Although I can't be with you today

If you can close your eyes and think

I'll be beside you in the kitchen

Wearing your jersey, over by the sink

I'll be with you in the bedroom

Waiting patiently on the bed

Just close your eyes and think of me

Relive our memory in your head

I'll stand by you in the bathroom

An odd place to meet

I'll smile at you so playfully

Letting you brush my teeth

I'll be your light in the darkness

Shining steady through and through

You only have to watch it glow

To know I am thinking of you

I'll be the rap music that you listen to

I'll be there in every verse

I'll laugh with you and rap with you

Even if I'm off beat but you sound worse

I'll be the air that cools you off

I'll be your warm embrace

I'll be the hand on your shoulder

Also the tender touch to your face

I'll be the clock on your nightstand

Reminding you of the times

Us shutting the world outside

We're in our own world - yours and mine

Though I am not there physically

As you live your life every single day

Just close your eyes and remember me

I will not be far away

I will never forget you........

Love's
Tantalizing Taste

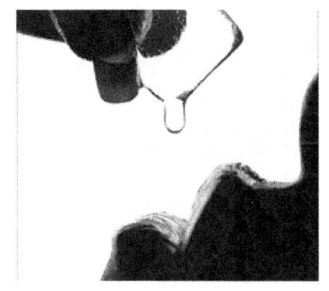

Premonition of Pleasure and Savory Secretions

Aroused...
From the lethal sound of your voice.
Stimulating, so dangerously
breathtaking, yet pure
innocent in its spirit.
Sexy as the body it possesses.

As you have made me feel
the intensity of your taste
for me, I also yearn for you
the same without delay.
The way you rub against me
my walls get so wet.

I can't help the feeling
of your fingers inside me.
My temperature rises
and emotions explode.

Feel ....

The warmth of my hands
caressing the muscular
physique of your body.
Licking you from the tip
of your earlobes softly down
the sides of your neck.
Tasting your neck
so sweet, so soft, so smooth.

Maneuvering my tongue down
towards your chest, to the creases
of your hips, to the inner segment
of your thighs, up across your navel
landing to my final destination
the sector I desire the most.

Finally reaching pure bliss.
Watching as you tremble
and bite your lip, feeling your hands
caressing through my head
The softness of each fingertip.

Taste….

So sweet, so enticing, potent!

Feeling you quiver
tremor with pleasure
from the stroke of my hands
massaging, the flickering of
my tongue at your crown's point
sampling a portion of
your uncontrollable urge.

You tell me not to stop
you want more
I continue to let my wet
lips explore you abundantly
savoring every taste making
you want me furthermore.

My mouth can feel raging pulses
boiling, you're ready to explode.
Eagerly awaiting my treat, you release
your savory secretions generously, on me.

Prisoner to Love

Take my hand please lead the way
Tell me everything you want to say
Confess your love softly in my ear
It's everything I'm longing to hear

In the darkness of the night
Be my moon shine your light
In the brightness of the sun
Show me that I am the only one

Slowly kiss my lips and touch my skin
Bringing out emotions deep within
Pull me close to you and hold me near
You're my drug for pain and fear

Break in my heart tear down that wall

It's time for me to watch hatred fall

I've been held captive can't you see

Cut my scorned ropes and set me free

Strip me of my guards so tight

You'll find I won't put up a fight

Release my soul held deep within

Set free now ready to let love begin

Seduce You With Words

Do you feel them baby?

Gently touching your face

Tracing the lines of your sexy lips

Flowing down your neck

Do you feel them gently

Unbuttoning your shirt

Rubbing across your chest

With teasing hands and warm strokes

Leaving finger prints of desire

Do you feel the pleasure of my wet lips

Kissing you intensely and deeply

Tongue dancing with tongue

Twirling in lustful tangos

The scent of my passion now

Satisfies your heated desire

The sweet drink of my urges

Quenching your thirst

Are my words seducing you

Do you feel the enticement

From my wet secret place

Surrounding you grasping you

Pulling you deeper inside me

Are the waves of passion

Floating over you now

As you drown in my love

Higher, hotter, stronger, sweeter

Until all you feel is lust

I am stroking you with my words

Did you feel ...

My touch?

Soaked

Does this mean I am drenched with water?

Or could this be how I get from
the thought of your touch
the tip of your tongue running
slowly up my moist thighs or
the power of your hands grabbing
my body
Now there is so much

My legs are quivering,
my mouth is moaning,
I am lusting for your body
on top of mines
for you to taste and be satisfied
lost from my love
exploring, touching, teasing
My body is so slippery
shivering with emotional bliss

You got me twisting

Dripping wet
I feel you as you are
pausing deep inside me
pulling out and thrusting back in
Feeling your sensations
deep inside me
moans of pure delight and ecstasy

Whisper into my ear
intense words to make weak
Looking into my eyes
with a mysterious provocative gaze
sends mystical showers of
electrifying thrills
throughout my entire body
To feel your flames
full of energy full of heat

Burning like no end

Cause you make my erotic
senses elevate
taking me higher and higher
than I have ever been

Touching my soul
Your body guiding me
in directions so divine
that takes control of
my sanities within

Impulses are escalating
Fused in the heat
of passionate tenderness
existing this moment
Crying out in anguished
bliss

Panting

Screaming for more

Feeling you rage with

passion and desire

so intense

Spreading my legs apart

tightening with every thrust as

you go deeper hitting the right spot

Waterfalls are gushing

I just can't get enough of

You

Laying in your arms

waves subside

flames dwindling

Reality sets in

Our bodies....

Soaked

Tongue of Passion

In a dark room, I feel your tender
lips whispering in my ear
Laying my delicate body down,
feeling the burn of your flames
from your tongue,
caressing the outline of
my neck with a desire surreal....

Your tongue, so passionate
so lustful,
Indulging in its craving,
Stimulating...purely intoxicating
Your tongue, boiling with
electrifying desire, igniting with delight...

My vulva is pulsing,
my breasts are perked
from the peak of your saturated tongue
passionately spiraling my navel
down to the middle of my luscious peach.

Can you taste it, my sweet drink?

Consume all my nectar,
my tasty flows from your hungry
tongue, devouring so deep
as if I was your banquet
and you can't get enough to eat.
Placing me on your plate of ecstasy.

There's something more intimate
with the way you deliver your
tongue emotionally.
So charming, so sweet
yet proving your masculinity.

The smoothness of your lips
touching the creases of my inner
thighs is about to send me
past an delusional state
of mind. From your lips
to mines, I
feel its presence
performing mind
blowing intimate kisses.

I am loving you between my legs
and from the motions of your
mouth I can tell you love this caramel
delight. I'd never had it like this before
so soft and amazingly warm.

Your tongue stroking me so
slowly, reaching the very depths
of my core. You have me throbbing
wanting more, pulsating with the
smooth rhythm you bestow.

Making me weak, so vulnerable
helpless, drowning from its power
seducing my mind with every
wave and twist. I've dreamt about it
and now feel its potency.

Stronger than a drug
but now my drug.

I'm so addicted.

Trusting

Love is what we all search,
Search in heart of others
We all want to be loved
Loved by others

Time is what we all need
Need to be self pleased
Pleased so that we can love each other
Pleased by others

Trust is what we all seek
Want to be trusted and to be believed
Trust is better than love

Trust grows up with time spent with others
Trust need both time and love
And for me trust is still maturing

Trust in my words...

Trust is hard to give and hard to gain.

It is the foundation to building love in a relationship, because if there is no trust then there is no love therefore you will doubt anything and everything your partner may say to you.

It definitely takes time to build. Let someone prove themselves to you before you give your all. Does that mean you start off by not trusting? No, because you have to start somewhere.

Remember people do change over time. Learning that lesson taught me that in life, there are no guarantees that someone could be and remain trustworthy.

Also remember that trust and respect goes together like chicken with hot sauce!

You can't have one without the other. If they broke your trust, they betrayed you. In betrayal there is a lack of respect, so in my words a person doesn't respect you if they betrayed you. Just saying.

But looking at the fact that no one is perfect in life you can choose to forgive them, if you can whole-heartedly forgive them and put it behind you.

Never underestimate the power someone has to change with determination and prayer, honest prayers from the heart asking for forgiveness and personal growth.

I'm learning everyday how to let go and believe again. It's not an easy task to accomplish when trust had been broken so many times. This was not advice to anyone, it was simply me expressing my views on trust. Much Love!!!!

Her Beauty

Staring upon this amazing
vision lying on my pillow
Lit from the moonlight
of my bedroom window
Wrapped within my loving arms
she is my life my precious charm

I gently touch her luscious lips
so soft and moist maybe a lil red
She brought me to life when
all hope was gone and faith was dead
She restored my heart when it was lost
melting away pain that was coated by frost

Gazing at her breasts so firm and strong
I know that her love could not be wrong
Life is beautiful watching her every breath
At first sight I knew she wasn't like the rest

Amazed by angelic eyes staring into mine
She fills my body as if it was potent wine
I close her eyes and seal with gentle kisses
Thanking God nightly
for granting my wishes

Until tomorrow night my love..

Between Us

We've been held apart
by fate for so long,
we hesitate when our bodies
are finally allowed to touch
afraid of the punishment
we've previously received.

Realizing we're alone
the passion we've held back
for so long is released and we
crash into each other like a
tsunami on the shore.

Physically
I feel you pushing
me hard into the wall
but mentally
we are knocking it down.

Lips fuse together in heated
lust, wanting this for so long.
No more!

The only thing in my mind
is you and me on yours.
I can tell as your hands explore me
there is nothing else beyond this.

We never know how much time we get
so we must make the most of it.
Although we seem to be going so fast
it doesn't seem rushed at all.

Bodies entwined you look into my
eyes and I know we may never
have this moment again. But for now
living this once is enough. We give our all.

Emotionally high
that's where we are now
Ooh this moment, right here
This moment...THIS FEELING!

Then it's gone...

What You Do To Me

It's your eyes that electrify me
Your lustful voice causes me to melt
One look at you immobilizes me
An emotion I've never ever felt

Can't help but stare
At those sexy brown eyes
Can't help but get so wet
See you give me butterflies

I want to say thank you
For the things you do
Stimulating sparks of desire
When I hear you say I love you

Can't help but go insane
For you and only you
These paralyzing emotions
Are honest and true

Longing to feel your kiss
From those soft sexy lips
When we part I'm bitter
From the love I miss

With feelings like this
Intensity at best
My erotic visions of us
Cannot cease to rest

As you lick my lips
Down to my neck
My body becomes paralyzed
As if I have just wrecked

Slow and delicious
The power of your touch
Pleasure and pain
From you I want so much

You toss me on top
Cause you love when i ride
Slowly picking up speed
I feel you gorging inside

As you shove in harder
You cause me to stutter
Hitting that one sensitive spot
Oh I can't go no further

Like a million orgasms
In just one kiss
See what you do to me
Pure pleasure and emotional bliss

Shivering sensations
Up and down my spine
An endless enchantment
Forever in this heart of mine

Deep

Trembling sweaty hands
Slide slowly delicately along
Your lightly oiled shaft
Hard and strong

Gently opening my lips
Guiding you with finger tips
Entering slowly with precision
With a purpose for this mission

Eyes water in hesitation
Swallows hard in anticipation
Running slowly over my teeth
Just a little further

You're down so deep

I begin to tighten up and tense
Tasting swallowing oily scent
Knowing you are there and ready
Releasing it quick as my throat holds steady

A Love So Sweet

~What you mean to me ~

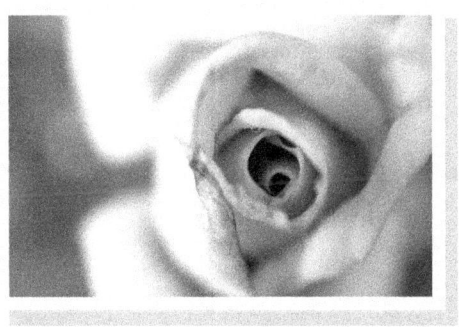

Your smile is so adorable

Touches are so endearing

Smart, funny, and wonderful

I love your laugh and

Your sick perverted jokes

But this is what I love

About you most

Because you are so real

So real I want you

But I can't have you

I'm missing you

Every moment I wake

All these emotions

Are about to explode

Nothing get accomplished

without a single thought of you

I was scared to love

But not with you

I set aside all my fears

Thrown them all away

You brought out a new me

Forever here to stay

To be the best I can be

My love for you

Never ending

Never changing

There's no denying

You're my best friend

Best I ever had

When I hear your voice

My days turn great

And smiles turn bright

You have my heart

And there's no returns

Here I stand

Patiently waiting for yours

After you realize

I am like no other

Yes real love

To my surprise

I was hypnotized

By them sexy brown eyes

You will never hear

More true and

Honest words

When I say

I'm in love with you

Forever in my dreams, a love so true

The flame of passion never dies

if the commitment to it never ends.

Passion a word which involves

so many feelings;

I feel it when we touch,

I feel it when we kiss,

I feel it when I look at him.

He is my passion, my one true love

Passion best described

When I'm about to see him,

the ache in my stomach

after I just left him.

Passion is the pain of him not in my life

Passion is what my love is for him.

Remembering love is the greatest
joy, and losing love is the hardest
pain. But memories of the sweetest
love is worth the heartache.

Thank you for reading some of my writings. This was my first collection so look for more to come.

This last one I want to leave you with is one that describes the importance of living for love.

Life can be short. Never forget the one who loves you the most, treats you right, but mainly appreciating what they do just for you.

Make it last, and most of all ...

Keep it Sexi Baby!!!

Destinee Love

A Love Lost

When I got home that night my husband was in the bedroom. I walked over to him and said we need to talk about something. He sat staring at the television quietly. I observed the hurt in his eyes, as we have had this talk plenty times before.

Suddenly I froze, I didn't know how to tell him I wanted him to leave and this time for real. But I had to let him know what was on my mind, I didn't want to be with him anymore. I raised the topic calmly. He didn't seem to be bothered by my words, instead he softly asked me why? I avoided the question. He yelled I always do this to him, and never give him a valid reason why I want to tear us apart.

That night we didn't speak to each other. Inside I was dying. I knew he wanted to know if there was someone else or just not happy anymore. I couldn't give him a valid answer even if I tried. I just didn't love him anymore. So I thought. With a deep sense of guilt, I couldn't sleep at all.

By the time I awoke he was gone. The man who had spent eight years of his life with me had become a stranger. I felt sorry for wasting his time, but everything we had in the beginning was now lost.

The next day, I came home very late and found a letter from him at the table. I was so tired I went straight to bed telling myself I was going to read it the next day. When I woke up, I forgot all about it and went straight to work. I wasn't in the right frame of mind to read it right away.

~In the beginning our relationship was very exciting, and passionate. Over time and many arguments, we became distant. I felt neglected and he felt unheard. Maybe the feelings were mutual, we just never talked about it. He used to be such a gentleman always giving me compliments, or holding my hand in times of need. He would even sneak kisses to me surprisingly, just because.

One day at work, I received a phone call from him asking if we could do one last thing before we had called it quits. He asked if we could go on another first date. I thought the idea was crazy but I agreed. We were going out the next night at the very spot we had our first dinner.

It was so beautiful. It was just as if we were on our first date all over again. I couldn't believe the emotions that were running through me that very moment. It was as if we were ourselves again. He was so sweet, the man I remember. And I was the love of his life, still. He had arranged for us to share a quiet dance together. Standing there in his arms everything felt so right. When the night was over, he had taken me home just like he did on our first date.

Gently giving me a kiss on the cheek, he said I would see him again soon. In my mind I was hoping he wouldn't leave, but he did. He was so amazing, our first date had been relived.

Sitting at the table in amazement it had all hit me, my life with him was never dull. We just didn't take time to value what mattered the most, intimacy and understanding in our relationship. It wasn't that we didn't love each other because it was clearly there. I raced over to the telephone to call him back over to talk, but no answer. I will just wait for him to return my call, it shouldn't take long if he'd seen it was me.

In the meantime,

I stumbled across his letter on the table. I had forgotten all about it until now. As I opened the letter I realized it was the very first one I had wrote him confessing my love. I couldn't believe he had it all this time. Seeing my feelings expressed for him on this paper really made me realize this he was my true love. I was not suppose to give up so easily. I'm not sure how he managed to keep this away from me without me knowing, but it took my breath away.

I needed him so badly right now. I needed to tell him how sorry I was, how selfish of me to not realize that relationships were not perfect. It takes hard work, and dedication. I had simply given up before giving it a chance.

I called once more this time leaving a voice message telling him to come straight over no matter the time if he wanted to because I had something important to tell him. Surely he would return my call now.

I decided to go ahead and rest since we both had a long evening. I'm sure if I didn't hear back from him tonight, we would definitely be talking tomorrow.

I had so many emotions racing through my head. I wondered what he was thinking, what he was doing, or if he was even thinking about me. As I drifted off to sleep with a smile on my face, I couldn't wait to see his once more. For now,

I will just imagine his warm arms comforting me.

That call never came.

It was two in the morning when I received the call that he was being taken to a local hospital. He was hit by a car two blocks away from my house. From the direction he was coming, tells a story he was on his way back to me.

Rushing out the door numb, barely conscience I had to get there to him. To be there by his side until he came home to us—a "new" us.

When I got there I rushed into his room to speak to him. I didn't know how bad it really was until I got there. I couldn't breathe! As I looked upon him wrapped in bandages from head to toe all I could think about is they have the wrong person this is not my love. The doctor came in to tell me how severe the accident was and all the injuries he sustained. He was brain dead. His life had

basically ended and there was nothing they could do but pull the plug. "NO"! I screamed. This can't be happening. The man I loved and cared for deeply! Just earlier we had shared precious time together. I leaned over my love crying my heart out to please wake up, I loved him too much I couldn't let him go. I refused!

Staring at him, he slightly opened his eyes to gaze directly into mines. It was the most amazing gaze that could have lasted forever, but it didn't. With a look of passionate love and sorrow he slowly escaped into a world with no more pain.

They did everything they could to save him, but his injuries were too severe. What am I supposed to do? How do I live, how can I go on! We never got the chance to tell each other how we felt, or what we wanted. Deep pain is now piercing my soul. Forever I will suffer never forgetting he was real love, true love, my love, Lost.

If you truly love someone, don't wait till tomorrow to let them know, because that next day may never come.

The smallest details in your life is what matters the most in a relationship. It is not the mansion, the car, property, or riches of the world. These elements create an environment conducive for happiness, but can be destruction within.

So find time to be your partner's friend, lover, and confidant. Whatever it may take to do the little things for each other that builds intimacy, and an unbreakable bond of love and trust. Most relationships fail because people don't take the time to rebuild when situations arise causing walls to collapse.

Restore and Rebuild!!! Love, Destinee

www.ingramcontent.com/pod-product-compliance
Lightning Source LLC
Chambersburg PA
CBHW072200280526
45788CB00002B/812